Me
and my
Newt

Pippa Goodhart

Illustrated by David Mostyn

Monday 3rd March

School:

Miss Saunders says we've got to write a journal. We've got to write down any interesting things that happen between now and midnight on Friday.

I asked, 'Miss, what if nothing interesting happens?'

She said, 'Knowing you, Carl Parsons, something interesting is bound to happen.'

She said that five minutes ago and nothing exciting has happened so far, so I'll write about big Ben Cox.

He's just tipped pencil-sharpenings down my neck! I shoved him with my elbow but Miss Saunders saw me. She told me off.

Ben's always getting me into trouble. He bumps into me and makes me drop things. He calls me, 'Titch!' just loud enough for the other children to hear, but not the teachers. And he leans on me. I hate that worse than anything!

I think I've got a dent in my head from his elbows!

I wish I could shrink Ben and lean on him!

I'm not going to moan about Ben for five days. I'll write down a joke instead.

What happens if you walk under a cow?

You get a pat on the head!

Kate from next door told me that joke. She's my friend.

Home:

When I got home today Mum had bought me a sweater. It had my age on the label, but it was far too big.

Mum put her hands on her hips and said, 'You're very small for your age, Carl!'

I know I am. Ben keeps telling me! Then Mum got all worried.

'Perhaps I'm not feeding you the right foods,' she said. 'I'll get you something special when I go shopping tomorrow.'

Good! I hope it's muffins and doughnuts to build me up!

Bedtime update:

Kate and I found something in the pond in her garden.

There was a kind of rainbow-coloured, dark patch on the water. It was oil. I think it must have come from the garage next door. Kate saw a bit of the oil suddenly rippling along. She said, 'It's a snake!' but it wasn't.

I found a stick and fished a lizardy thing out of the pond.

It was all gungy with oil. I got gungy with oil too. So did Kate. It stuck to everything.

The little lizard must have been coming up to breathe some air and got oil instead of air. That must feel horrible.

Kate said, 'He might die!'

I've seen on television about birds dying because of oil on beaches. Rescue people wash the birds with detergent and try to save them. I thought we could try that too. I carried the lizard home.

Mum shouted when she saw our black hands, 'Don't touch anything!' Then she noticed the lizard and started saying, 'Oh, poor little thing.'

We put the lizard in a box and Mum drove us to the vet's.

The vet said, 'This little chap's a Common Newt.' She wore tweedy clothes as thick as carpets and she called our newt 'common', but I liked her.

She said, 'Good for you!' to us for bringing the newt to her instead of trying to clean him at home.

She washed the newt with special stuff for cleaning off oil.

I asked her, 'Can we keep the newt?'

She said, 'Yes, but only while the newt is getting better'. Mum made a face when she heard that!

The vet said to feed the newt on worms and flies. The flies have to be alive! She said that the newt should be better by Saturday.

'Then you must put the little chap back where you found him, if the pond's been cleaned.'

So I've got something to write about in my journal after all!

Mum found the old fish bowl. Kate and I got water and stuff from another pond and put it all in the bowl. We even put a stone in to make an island. The vet said that newts don't want to be in water all the time.

After Kate went home, I caught flies off Mum's pot plants. She never sprays them, so there were loads, all yummy and alive! I put the flies into the bowl.

I hope my newt likes them. Hey – I've just had an idea. I think I'll call my newt, Minute! He is very small and he is my newt, so it's just right.

Note: Tell Kate about the name tomorrow.

Tuesday 4th March

School:

Kate thinks that Minute is a great name.

Big Ben pushed in and wanted to know what we were talking about. I told him I've got a wild animal for a pet.

'What,' he asked, 'a tiger, or a crocodile or something?'

'No,' I said, 'a newt.'

Ben laughed. He said that newts were small and stupid and that made them just the right kind of pet for me. Typical! I told him that his dog, Clint, was really ugly and just the right kind of pet for him.

Ben called me Titch and leaned on me. I'll get him back for that.

Home:

Most of the flies have gone from the bowl. Minute must have eaten them. I think that means he's happy. I've found a book that says that unhappy animals don't eat.

I've got Minute walking up my arm now. He walks with his elbows out, like a wind-up toy. He feels tickly but nice. He's soft and not slimy at all.

I'll put him back now and get some worms for his tea.

The book says that worms come up out of the ground when it rains. Birds stamp on the ground to sound like rain when they want to catch a worm. Note: Try stamping like birds to sound like raindrops. Do the worms come up?

Mum's just come back from shopping. 'I've bought something special for you,' she said.

Guess what? It's just a boring old packet of beans!

'They cost a lot of money, so I hope they work!' said Mum.

I wonder if they will? I wonder what they taste like?

Bedtime update:
I found out what the beans taste like – *yuk, yuk, yuk!*

Mum tried to make them look like normal beans on toast. She mixed them with ketchup to make them red instead of white. But they smell terrible. They pong like six-million-year-old cheesy bits from between your toes!

I held my nose and put some in my mouth. I swallowed them down quickly, but there were still a few left on the plate. No way was I going to eat them!

I could hear Mum coming. I scraped the last beans off my plate and into the nearest thing – the fish bowl.

They floated, slowly, down through the water, looking like big, pale maggots.

Minute swam over to have a look. I wonder if he'll try and eat one?

Note 1: Clean out Minute's bowl first thing in the morning.
Note 2: Never ever eat gringle beans again!
Note 3: Yes, stamping on the ground does make the worms come up. I got loads.

Wednesday 5th March

Minute has grown! I couldn't believe it when I came downstairs this morning. I thought the curved bowl must be making him seem bigger than he was, but it wasn't. He really has grown!

Now I'm sitting here and wondering – was it those gringle beans?

The beans have all gone. I think Minute must have eaten them all. That's amazing! A few beans are a lot for a little newt.

It's like me eating a pile of food that would fill a wheelbarrow! Perhaps he's just grown because he's eaten so much and not because the beans are special?

But yesterday Minute was only eight centimetres long. I've just measured him now and he's fifteen centimetres long! That's a lot of growing in one night.

My book says that Great Crested Newts can grow to fifteen centimetres long. It's against the law to catch and to keep them.

Minute is just a Common Newt. It's not good to take them away from the wild either. That's why he will have to go back to the pond on Saturday. The book says that Common Newts are only ten centimetres long.

Perhaps I've got the biggest Common Newt in the world! He's an uncommon Common Newt! He's beautiful. He's a greeny-brown colour on top and orange underneath. He has dark spots all over.

Note 1: If I'd eaten the beans and grown as much as Minute, then I'd be too tall to stand up in our house!

Shall I try the beans again? Is it worth the yuk taste to look down on big Ben?

Note 2: Must find a bigger bowl for Minute.

School:

At lunch time, I wanted to tell Kate about Minute and the beans. Nosy Ben came along so we couldn't talk.

'Go away, Ben!' I told him, but he wouldn't go away.

So Kate and I made a Ben-proof den where we could be private. We've crawled into the hedge at the end of the playground.

Ben's too big to fit through. Now he's stuck outside wondering what I'm writing about him.

The good news is that Kate says she's got a big glass tank I can borrow for Minute. We're going to use the den again when we want to get away from Ben. *Ha ha* to Ben!

Update:

The den isn't so brilliant after all. Kate and I climbed into it at afternoon break. Ben poked us with sticks through the hedge. We couldn't get away. When we got out, he leaned on me. I stamped on his toe. Then the bell rang.

Note: Never poke an animal in a cage. It's horrible and it's not fair.

Home:

Kate brought her tank round and we've put it in my bedroom. I think Minute likes it, but it's hard to tell. He's grown another two centimetres since this morning!

I can really see his face now. It's a strange face. He doesn't smile or laugh, or cry, or make any noise. He doesn't even blink. He's just looking at me. He seems a bit sad. Perhaps he doesn't like getting big. Perhaps he doesn't like being indoors. Perhaps he wants to be with other newts.

The book says that in March, newts go to ponds to find other newts. It's March now – but he'll be back out in the wild in two days' time.

Note 1: Fix a mirror to one end of Minute's tank. That way he'll see himself and think there's another newt to be his friend. He might think the tank is bigger too. I wish it really was bigger.

Got to go now – Mum's calling me for tea. It's pizza and my slice will have gringle beans on it.

'I'm going to build you up, Carl,' Mum says.

I'll save the beans for Minute. He liked them yesterday. I want to know if they will make him grow even bigger. But I don't think a newt could get much bigger.

Thursday 6th March

Help! Minute's grown again!

I'm trying my plan to make Minute happier. I've put Dad's shaving mirror at the end of Minute's tank, but Minute isn't impressed. He somehow knows that the newt swimming in the mirror isn't real.

He doesn't take any notice of the mirror. He just flips around and paddles the other way. Then he flips again because he's at the other end of the tank already. He's just flip, paddle, flip, paddle, all the time. Even this tank is too small for him now.

It's interesting that Minute's so clever. Perhaps he's clever enough to learn to talk. I'd be famous if I had a giant, genius, talking newt!

The book doesn't say anything about newts talking, but the book doesn't know everything. I can tell it's never met a Common Newt like Minute.

Note 1: Plan talking lessons for Minute. Get Kate to help.

Note 2: Give Minute a swim in the bath. Could he come swimming with me? I'd like to swim with him. People do swim with dolphins.

School:

Ben's just stolen my packet of crisps.
He held it above my head and I
jumped, but I couldn't reach it. He
threw some crisps into the air and
caught them in his mouth, like a seal
with a fish.

They were cheese and onion
flavour – my favourite. Ben ate them
all. I'll get him back for that.

Kate has an idea. She says we should pretend Minute is a sausage dog and take him for a walk. Minute is now the same size and shape as a small sausage dog.

Kate says she'll make him some brown ears to wear, but I don't think it's a good idea.

I don't think I can take Minute swimming either. People would stare. Minute is quite a private kind of newt.

I'm glad he's going back to his pond on Saturday. But before that I'm going to try and get him to talk. I want him to tell me what it's like living in a pond and under logs. That would be interesting.

Home:

Minute's grown again! He's living under my bed now.

I'm worried about putting him back in the garden. Will the other newts be friends with him? Or will they not like him because he's so big?

Kate and I tried to get Minute to talk. We said things very slowly and made our mouths very big, but Minute didn't make any sound back.

I don't think he's stupid. He's just a newt and newts don't talk.

Mum's busy cooking downstairs –
I wonder what this time?! While she's
out of the way, Kate and I are going to
give Minute a swim.

Kate's filling the bath now and
Minute is waiting with me. It's a pity
he's too big to fit on my lap any more.

Later:

Minute liked swimming in the bath.
He paddled around with his elbows
sticking out.

But then Mum called us for tea and I couldn't lift him out! Perhaps he grew some more in the bath? Kate and I had to sling towels under each end of him to haul him out. Poor Minute!

Kate said, 'He's as big as a crocodile!'

He does look quite like a crocodile who's lost his teeth and had his nose squashed.

Then Kate said, 'Let's show him to Ben!'

That's a brilliant idea! Then Ben won't be able to sneer at newts for being small.

Kate's going home now and Minute is back under my bed. I've given him my duvet to hide under – I hope he feels cosy. I'll have to sleep wearing jumpers and socks tonight so that I don't freeze.

It was pasta with beans for tea. Mum is cross with the beans. She says it's an outrage that they cost such a lot. She says that what the packet says, about the beans making you grow, is nonsense.

But then she hasn't seen Minute in the last two days! I gave my beans to Minute again. I want him as big as possible when Ben sees him.

Note 1: Invite Ben to my house.

Friday 7th March

School:

At morning break, I asked Ben if he'd like to come to my house. He leaned on me and asked, 'Why?'

I told him, 'To show you that newts aren't small and boring.'

Ben did a sneery laugh and said, 'OK!'

Now I'm sitting here writing this and trying not to smile too much. I know that if I look at Kate and she looks at me, we'll both laugh. Then Ben will guess that we're up to something.

I can't wait for the end of school!

Home:
Ben walked home with Kate and me. We made him wait downstairs with Mum while we got things ready in my bedroom.

Minute had grown even more! He's enormous!

Kate had a brilliant, horrible idea. She found an arm from an old broken doll of hers. She drew on the arm with a red felt pen and put it near Minute's mouth. It looked really horrible. It looked as if Minute had chewed an arm off a baby.

I hope that Minute didn't understand what Kate had done. Minute would never ever hurt anyone. But Ben deserved a scare.

We called Ben upstairs.

I told him, 'Don't be afraid. It's only a newt!'

He said, 'I'm not afraid of a weedy little newt!'

He pushed past me into my room, stopped, and stepped back – on to my toe! Typical!

'It's a cccc-crocodile!' he said. Then he fainted, *Thunk!*, and fell on to my bedroom floor! Brilliant!

Kate and I got Minute back under the bed and called for Mum. Mum fussed around Ben. He opened his eyes and whimpered about a man-eating crocodile.

'Poor lad!' said Mum, 'I wonder what's the matter?'

Kate was laughing. I just liked looking down on Ben for once. I could have leaned on him but I didn't.

Mum gave us both a look, so we helped to get Ben downstairs.

We sat him on a chair. Mum gave him a drink and a biscuit. She put her hand on his forehead and said, 'Are you feeling any better, sweetheart?' She called big Ben Cox, 'sweetheart'!

Ben's mother came to fetch him. We told her about Ben fainting when he saw a newt. Ben's mum is big. She's huge! She looked down at Ben and called him a 'great dollop'. Ben looked small beside her. I felt quite sorry for him.

Note: Ask Ben to come round to play properly sometime.

Kate and Ben have gone now. I feel quite sad. I feel sad for Ben, even though he deserved what we did to him. And I feel sad for Minute.

Ben was scared just because Minute was big. He didn't even notice that Minute is beautiful and has friendly eyes. I'm going to help Minute get back to being a normal newt. Then I'm going to let him go home.

I'm sad for me too – I'll miss Minute. At least I've got Kate. Perhaps Ben can turn into a friend too – if he'll stop leaning on me!

Note 1: Don't feed any more beans to Minute. Will he shrink back?

Note 2: Put Minute back in the wild as soon as possible.

Note 3: Tell Ben I don't like being leaned on.

I wonder what's for tea. It doesn't smell of old socks. Please, anything but gringle beans!

Update:

Tea was normal fish and chips with no gringle beans – *hooray*!

Mum told me, 'You've eaten all but one of the wretched beans. I can't see any difference in you. I shan't waste my money on them again.'

Then she ruffled my hair, the way I hate, and she said, 'Anyway, who cares about being big or small? I love you just the way you are, sweety!' Thank goodness Kate and Ben didn't hear her saying that!

The very last bean was on my pudding. I hid it in my pocket.

When I went to get worms for Minute's supper, I buried the bean in the compost heap.

Minute is beside me on the bed now. He's resting his chin on my lap.

He only ate two small worms for supper. I think he's shrunk a little bit. I hope so. If he'll shrink back to newt size, then he can fit in with other newts and be happy.

I wish now that I'd never made Minute so big. I shouldn't have gone on making him bigger, just to scare Ben. I wish I hadn't.

They've got the oil out of the pond so Minute can go home.

Note: Get up early and take Minute outside before Mum and the others get up. He's got to be out of the room before Mum does her Saturday clean up!

Update at almost midnight:
I've been awake all night! I haven't slept because I've been thinking. If gringle beans make things grow gigantic, then could they be the kind of bean that's in *Jack and the Beanstalk*?

Maybe a giant bean plant is growing out of the compost heap right now?

I've had another thought too. What if the creepy-crawlies in the compost heap start to eat the bean?

It's been interesting having a newt-crocodile, but do I want a worm-snake?

Or a woodlouse-armadillo?

Or even a great, green, hopping frog-kangaroo?

I've just looked under my bed for Minute. He's disappeared!

I found him! He's back to being normal tiny newt size! I can hold him in my hand again. He's completely better, but he looks a bit worried.

He must feel as if the world around him has suddenly grown gigantic!

I wonder if Ben felt small when he saw huge Minute? If he did, then in a way, I did shrink big Ben!

I won't do it again, though. I'll take Minute back to his pond right now.

He can make friends with other newts and forget all about this strange week.

If I use my torch, I can find the hole in the hedge and get to Kate's pond through the shortcut. While I'm out there with my torch, I'll just take a peek at that compost heap too …

About the author

Do you ever look at ordinary things, and think, 'what if …'?

This story started when I moved a log at the end of our garden. There were newts living under the log. One baby newt was only a couple of centimetres long. I looked at it and thought, 'What if it grows to adult size, but doesn't stop there? What if it grows to crocodile size?!'

That thought grew too, into this story.